THE YOUNG ENTREPRENEURS' CLUB

GADGETS AND INVENTIONS

MIKE HOBBS

W
FRANKLIN WATTS
LONDON•SYDNEY

First published in 2012 by Franklin Watts

Copyright © Franklin Watts 2012
Franklin Watts
338 Euston Road
London NW1 3BH

Franklin Watts Australia
Level 17/207 Kent Street
Sydney, NSW 2000

Series Editor: Paul Rockett
Consultant: David Gray
Design: Simon Borrough
Picture Research: Diana Morris

Dewey number: 338.4'

ISBN: 978 1 4451 1054 7

Printed in China

Franklin Watts is a division of
Hachette Children's Books,
an Hachette UK company.

www.hachette.co.uk

Every attempt has been made to clear copyright. Should there be any inadvertent omission please apply to the publisher for rectification.

Picture credits: Alibi Productions/Alamy: 26; Alta G . www.alta-g.com <http://www.alta-g.com> : 27c, 27b; Amazing Kids. Amazing-kids.org: 13t; AVA the Elephant.www.avatheelephant.com: 33; RichardBakerWork/Alamy: 30; Christian Beloga/ Shutterstock: 12t; BKFK: 13; bloomua/Shutterstock: 41; Peter Brooker/Rex Features: 18; Michael D Brown/ Shutterstock: 40; Neil Dawson , courtesy of www. littleriot.co.uk <http://www.littleriot.co.uk> : 17t, 17b; Ashley van Dyke/Shutterstock: 22; Mark Elite/Aflo Co Ltd/Alamy: 12b; Sergil Figurny/Dreamstime: 14; Guilu/Shutterstock: 8; Gum Drop. www.gumdropbin. com <http://www.gumdropbin.com> : 29l; Jon Enoch Photography, 29r; Reed Kaester/Corbis: 34; Bruce Kluckhorn/TimeLIfe/Getty Images: 23t; Tony Kyriacou/Rex Features: 15; LHB/Alamy: 32; Zern Liew/ Shutterstock: 38b; Bruce Longren/istockphoto: 16; ManCans. www.man-cans.com <http://www.man-cans. com> : 37t, 37b; Joanna Montgomery courtesy of www.littleriot.co.uk <http://www.littleriot.co.uk> : 17; Noiral /Dreamstime: 25c; Denis Opolja/Shutterstock: 36; Pet Lawn. www.internationalpetsolutions.com <http://www.internationalpetsolutions.com> : 21t, 21b; John Powell/Bubbles/Alamy: 28; Rex Features: 39; Alex Roe/Shutterstock: front cover inset; Alex Roz/Shutterstock: 7; Shamleen/Shutterstock: 20; Courtesy of Shell LiveWIRE: 19; Mihai Simonia <http://www.shutterstock.com/gallery-93635p1. html> /Shutterstock: front cover bg; Radin Strojek/ Shutterstock: 38t; St3fano/Dreamstime: 11; ThinkLite. com: 25t; trunki. www.magmatic.co.uk <http://www. magmatic.co.uk> : 9; Rolf Vennenbernd/Corbis: 35; wavebreakmedia ltd/Shutterstock: 5; Wikipedia: 22c; Woody Stock/Alamy: 10; All courtesy of www. wristies.com <http://www.wristies.com> : 31; Viktor Zadorozhni/Shutterstock: 24.

CONTENTS

8 The business of inventing

10 What makes a successful entrepreneur?

12 Finding the spark

14 Getting funding

16 Developing your idea

18 Researching your market

20 Improving the design

22 Getting legal protection

24 Developing your financial plan

26 Building a team

28 Leading from the front

30 Developing your marketing plan

32 Getting known

34 Off with a bang!

36 Tracking sales and distribution

38 Turning problems into gains

40 So what's next?

42 Glossary

43 Further information

44 Index

The business of inventing

Life changing

The world's progress depends on new ideas – new inventions and gadgets make it easier to live our lives. Where would we be these days without mobile phones? They only came on the market in 1983, and didn't sell in large numbers for several more years. Can you imagine a world without them? The great thing about inventing is that you might be able to make a difference to people's lives. Think of the things you use in your daily life: someone will have invented it.

Inventing is a genuine business, and with the right idea and a good business plan, it can make you a lot of money.

Patents

Anyone can have an idea for an invention and many people apply each year for a patent. A patent is a legal document that gives you, and no one else, the right to make and sell your inventions. In applying for a patent you are looking to claim legal ownership of your idea. Not all of the patented ideas will get made however, but the information in the Facts box will show you that many people want to take part in the business of inventing.

CHALLENGE

Think of a recent gadget or invention. Write out three sentences stating why they are successful. Think about its function, and how it has been packaged and marketed.

Facts:

In 1883, there were 18,051 applications for patents through the UK office, and nearly twice that number (35,230) through the US office.

By 1988, there were just over 1,000,000 applications worldwide for patents for inventions.

In 2008, there were over 1,900,000 applications worldwide for patents for inventions. Of these, 22,465 were in the UK and over twenty times that number (456,106) in the US.

There were 47,806 patent applications for computer technology and 1,109 for management information technology inventions in 1990.

By 2007 both had increased massively – there were 145,282 patent applications for computer technology and 25,900 for management information technology inventions.

YOUR THOUGHTS

Do you think Rob was right to have faith in his invention? What would you have done differently to gain success more quickly?

Young Entrepreneur
Trunki

The whole process of inventing can take a long time from the first idea to final delivery of the product. In the case of Rob Law (above) and Trunki, his ride-on suitcase for children, it took about nine years. He first thought of his invention in 1997 when he was at university and entered a competition. He had seen how bored children can get at airports. He imagined what fun it would be for them if they could ride around on their suitcases – his prototype won the competition.

By 2003, Rob had worked for several companies as a product designer, and was ready to take the idea for Trunki further. He licensed the idea to a toy company who did very little with it for three years before going bust. So he decided to set up his own company, Magmatic, and make the product himself. Despite further setbacks, including a key factory in China going bust and a design fault causing the suitcase strap to break, he has been very successful. His company currently has a turnover of six million pounds, and is looking to reach ten million in the next two years. This shows that he was right to believe in his product and that it was worth the hard work and time that it took to make.

What makes a successful entrepreneur?

Necessary qualities

What is an entrepreneur? Someone who takes a financial risk investing in an idea in order to make a profit. The idea may be yours or it could be someone else's that you have adapted and improved. Wherever your idea comes from, you have to be the one who's going to try to find people to buy it. It should be something that is possible to make and sell at a profit. Of course not every idea hits the jackpot. You need to be sure you're ready to run the risk.

There are many qualities you need to be successful. It is important to have a real passion for what you're doing, and strong determination and persistence. Obviously you have to be bright, inventive and forward-thinking. For any new gadget or invention, you must show fine attention to detail. If you can match these with the ability to work hard, and understand what the public will like, then you'll be an entrepreneur.

CHALLENGE

Think of an invention that would help people learn to swim. Make a list of all the qualities that would be needed to make this invention successful. Tick those qualities that you have and then those that your friends have. Who would make the best entrepreneur out of you and your friends?

Inspiring Entrepreneur
Bill Gates

Everyone knows that Bill Gates (left), who founded Microsoft in 1975, is one of the wealthiest men in the world. But he didn't hit the jackpot straight away. Before Microsoft he started Traf-O-Data (1972), a computer system that gathered traffic data. It didn't take off, but it got him developing new computer software. Working with computer software seemed to be something he was good at, enjoyed doing and saw as being important for the future.

Gates had a vision of putting personal computers onto every office desk and into every home. He believed that it was the software and not the computer hardware that would be important for computer-users and that this would be where the money was.

The experience of Traf-O-Data, not just in software development but also in running a business, led the way to Microsoft, which now provides computer software packages for the majority of computers worldwide.

YOUR THOUGHTS

What do you think makes Bill Gates a successful entrepreneur?

Finding the spark

Something new

No-one can really say where the spark comes from, but you know when you've got it. It's that moment when you think of a great idea and wonder why no-one's done it before. There could be a very good reason. It may be that the technology has only just become available, perhaps as a result of another invention. Whatever it is, the light bulb goes on above your head and you're wondering if your idea could be the start of something big. You may have just dreamed up a breakthrough new gadget or invention.

X-ray glasses and flying cars may seem like fantasy ideas, but people are working hard to make them a reality.

Have a think . . .

Ideas can come from your experiences and what you see around you. You're out and about, maybe performing some task, and you realise that things would be so much simpler if they could be done in a different way. It helps if you have a practical mind, since most inventions are based on technology, but sometimes all you need is curiosity and the drive to follow things through.

Now what you need to do is to find out if you can make your invention, produce enough of it to sell, and gain the interest of the buying public. Almost two million people each year approach the stage of marketing their invention. Many millions more dream about doing so.

How do you make sure you become one of the inventors, and not just one of the dreamers? It's simple. This is when you need to start acting like an entrepreneur.

Young Entrepreneur
Cassidy Goldstein

Cassidy Goldstein (left) was eleven years old when she invented the Crayon Holder. Using crayons for a school writing project, Cassidy became frustrated by the crayons being worn down into tiny bits which were hard to use. She wanted something to help her hold the small crayon pieces so that she could continue to use them. She found a clear plastic tube that was designed to hold cut flowers and put the pieces of crayons into the tube. She was able to hold the tube as she would a new crayon or pencil — and the Crayon Holder was born!

It's a very simple idea, and it helps children learning to draw, protects their hands from getting dirty and extends the life of a crayon. To make the Crayon Holder widely available, Cassidy's father helped complete the patents forms and got deals with manufacturers, shops and businesses. The Crayon Holder is now available online, through catalogues, and large shops in the US like Wal-Mart.

YOUR THOUGHTS

Where did Cassidy's idea come from?

Getting funding

Costs for starting up

Once you have come up with your idea you are going to need some money to make it happen. You may need the money to build the prototype, which is when you turn the idea into an object. You may need it to test the materials or for further research. You should try and figure out how much you think you'll need and explore all the different places and people you can approach for money to help start a business, and become your backers.

Try friends and family first, before you try banks and other sources. Then begin working out a proper budget, including all the costs you'll have to pay. Be realistic about your sales, because anyone who invests in your invention will want to know the likely figures.

Loans, grants and prizes

You may be able to get a loan or a grant to start up a new business in your area to develop your invention. This is especially true for young entrepreneurs. Go to the local library or find out if grants or money are given to inventors like you by searching on the Internet. There may even be various prizes for new gadgets or inventions available. But otherwise, whoever you want to invest in your business will need some clear financial plans that they believe you've got a chance of achieving.

CHALLENGE

You've come up with an idea for waterproof socks. Research the costs involved in making a prototype and then write a list of people and places that could be suitable backers.

Young Entrepreneur
Kevin Scott

Kevin Scott (bottom right) invented a bendy bicycle that wraps itself round lampposts or poles so that it can be left securely. It's able to do this with a special ratchet system which transforms two parts of the bike from stiff to bendable. Once wrapped, a single bike lock can be passed through both tyres and the frame. The aim is to improve bike security and cause a decrease in the number of bikes that are stolen.

For this invention, Kevin won runner-up in the UK's Business Design Centre New Designer of the Year Award in 2010. He also received £500 to help with costs. But this is where the real process of finding proper start-up funding began. Kevin's particular aim has been to use the publicity from the award – and there was a lot of it – to find a backer (maybe a cycling enthusiast) to enable the bendy bike to go into full production.

YOUR THOUGHTS

What type of people do you think would be interested in helping Kevin fund the manufacturing of his bikes?

Developing your idea

From idea to object

Once you've got some money to start you off, you can begin to work out how you are going to put your brainwave for a gadget or invention into production. There can be quite a lot of difference between your first idea and your end product.

An early prototype might be built to a smaller scale than your final product.

Make a prototype

What you need to do is to develop a prototype of your invention. A prototype is a version of your product which can be tested to see if any changes are needed before it goes into production. You're not worried so much about how it looks at the moment, that will come later. You're focusing on how it works, and whether it's likely to keep working when it is used again and again.

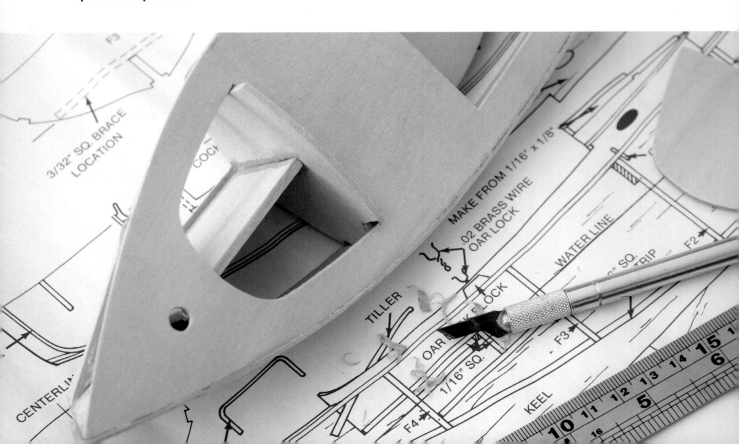

Young Entrepreneurs
Storymaker, Storyteller

Lee Murray, Natalie Montgomery, Joanna Montgomery and Neil Dawson (left) completed their award-winning Storymaker, Storyteller project while at university in Scotland. Its purpose was for a grandfather to pass on his memories to his grandson. They investigated different materials and technologies, old and new, to find the best way to record and play back family stories. They had to keep in mind the people who would be using the gadgets: the grandfather would find it easier to use technology that would be more familiar than the latest digital inventions.

As a result of the research, the idea developed to become two linked gadgets. The Storymaker is a small, handheld device for inserting slides and recording a story. The Storyteller is a mini desktop projector that plays the story while showing the slides in much smaller images than is usual. Together, they won Best End-to-End Design at the Seattle Expo in 2008.

YOUR THOUGHTS

How did thinking about who would be using the product affect the Storymaker, Storyteller?

Researching your market

Will people be interested?

OK, so you've got a good idea for an invention or gadget which might work, but will there be enough people to buy what you're selling? This is where market research comes in. Before you spend money bringing your idea to life, test to see whether there's a market. It doesn't have to cost the earth, as there are various cheap things you can do to find your market.

Asking people questions in the street is a form of primary research.

Primary and secondary research

There are two main types of research.

Primary research can involve walking round observing things or asking people questions to find out new information. You may want to approach people in the street and ask them questions. This will only be relevant to you if you want to sell your gadget to the public, and would like some feedback. If your prototype is ready, you could use it for demonstrations.

Secondary research involves finding information and facts in the library and on the Internet that already exist.

CHALLENGE

You've had an idea for an app that helps people look up family history records instantly. How would you set about researching the market?

Young Entrepreneur
ArtiCheke

Annika Erikson came up with the idea for ArtiCheke from her own experience of working in galleries and museums. ArtiCheke is an iPad app for artwork documentation that takes away much of the time-consuming duties of art gallery staff. Every new exhibition in a museum or gallery involves the movement of many pieces of art. All of the artwork has to be checked both before and after the exhibition in case anything has been damaged. Some exhibitions need more than 800 pieces of paper for insurance purposes and the paperwork would then have to be stored for several years afterwards.

Annika knew the market but checked with others within the industry to get their feedback. They agreed that digitising the art-checking process would be a good thing. The app has made the job paper-free, with the information easy to store and quickly searchable. This has made the work easier and quicker to perform and as a result, Annika's company won a Shell LiveWIRE ideas award in April 2011.

YOUR THOUGHTS

How did Annika know that there was a need for her invention?

Improving the design

Making it perfect

You've tested your prototype, researched your market and found some money to get you going. That's great, but now you have to use your research and make sure your idea really gets into shape. In other words there's still plenty to do before you can think about selling your product. You need to design your product (or get someone else to do it for you) so it looks as exciting as possible without taking away any of its ability to work.

CHALLENGE

The different screens of an app and how you navigate through them often start out designed as a wireframe. Have a look on the Internet to see a wireframe layout and use it as a template to improve the navigation of a familiar app.

So you have to try things out and see what you can do to improve your invention. Now's the time to work hard at developing your product – you must have it as close to perfect as you can when you decide to launch. This can mean delays which are hard to take because you know how fast the rate of change is in the world outside, and you're keen to move swiftly. However, it's very important that you take time to make your invention as attractive as possible.

Young Entrepreneurs
PetLawn

Dylan Balsz and Tilden Smith (right), from Orange County, California formed PetLawn in January 2011 while still at college, to market their new invention. It is a small patch of artificial grass which they describe as an indoor outhouse (toilet) for pets. When Dylan's family moved from a house with a lawn to an apartment with no garden, he was inspired to invent something which would help his dog go to the toilet without having to leave the house. The result was PetLawn, lined with pads that kill the smells and bags that absorb the waste.

There have been improvements to the design in two general areas that have helped them beat the competition. Since launching, they now offer extras such as cleaning solutions and replacement grass, bags and pads. These upgrades give customers more for a lower price and are extras that the competition doesn't offer. In addition, changes to the packaging design, making it brighter and more eye-catching, have attracted customers before they were even aware of these extras, adding to their success.

YOUR THOUGHTS

How are PetLawn's improvements a good thing?

Getting legal protection

Protecting your idea

One of the problems with inventing a sparkling new gadget is that someone else may pinch your idea. It's not impossible that they may have been thinking along the same lines at the same time. So you need to protect it by registering it as your idea. This is called applying for a patent. Once granted, you are protected by law, in the country where you applied (or group of countries if they are part of an agreement). It can take up to four years to grant, but no-one else can file a claim for that invention while you're waiting.

Applying for a patent is quite simple. You write to the office in your country (such as the UK Patent Office or the US Patent and Trademark Office) giving details of your invention, saying why it is new, how to make it and how it can be used. You can also apply to protect the design of your product (or, in the USA, apply for a design patent) and to protect its trademark or logo. You may have to pay an annual fee once the patent has been granted in order to keep the patent.

CHALLENGE

Think of an idea for a new invention. Write a letter to the Patent Office stating what your invention is, why it is new, how to make it and how it can be used.

Young Entrepreneur
Makin' Bacon

Abbey Fleck (above) from St Paul, Minnesota invented the Makin' Bacon dish (right) with her father back in 1993, as a way of trying to keep the bacon cooking above the fat rather than in it. They applied for a patent which they were granted in 1996. In 1997, they successfully settled a patent infringement suit against a Pennsylvania company that had begun to sell a similar device. When Wal-Mart ordered 100,000 of the dishes, her grandfather was able to take out a start-up loan to take care of manufacturing.

Where Abbey and her team had an advantage was simple: Abbey's age, as she was eight years old when she invented Makin' Bacon. They were able to use that to get loads of publicity. US TV shows rushed to feature her – *Oprah*, *David Letterman* and the *Today Show* among others. Newspapers and magazines weren't far behind, including *People Magazine* and *Good Housekeeping*. When such a story was combined with so simple a product and a protected patent, there was no shortage of investors.

YOUR THOUGHTS

Why did applying for a patent early help Abbey to develop a successful product?

Developing your financial plan

Getting the figures right

It won't matter how good your invention is if you can't make money on it. Now's the time to take your financial plan and develop it; you need to make further plans to show where your profits are coming from. You'll also have to ensure good cash flow, keeping a regular supply of money coming in. You will stand more chance of getting long-term investment if you've got a proper financial plan, showing what the backers will get in return and when they'll get it. The details you'll need to include in this plan are:

• Amount you need to invest in equipment, such as the machinery for making your invention.
• Amount you'll have to pay on weekly running costs, such as salaries and rent.
• Other estimated special costs – this may include money for development and publicity.
• Predicted sales for your first year.

Also include the likely date of first payment to investors. Include all the costs you'll have to pay and be realistic about your likely sales. Remember, your profit is the money you bring in minus your costs.

CHALLENGE

There's lots of excitement about your invention for child-friendly non-toxic paints. People are starting to place orders. How do you get the money to make these sales?

Young Entrepreneurs

ThinkLite

ThinkLite is a new way of saving energy and money on lighting for large buildings and offices. They make energy-saving light fittings, inventing light bulbs, switches and circuits that adapt the original fixtures and fittings of each office or building.

Founder Dinesh Wadhwani (right) says that he got the idea for ThinkLite from a simple energy-efficient light bulb advertisement. He started the company in Framingham, Massachussetts in 2009, determined to win customers by the savings he could offer them, not just because it was good for the environment. So far, so good – but the lighting systems had to be extremely energy efficient in order to help their customers make good savings.

It needed careful financial planning. Dinesh improved the product by using private laboratories in Germany. Then he brought in the components from Korea and everything was assembled in China. So far, ThinkLite claims it is saving its customers between 50% and 80% of their annual lighting bill. ThinkLite's fee is roughly 40% of the total savings a client will make over two or three years. So everybody wins, and the company has already gained widespread media coverage.

YOUR THOUGHTS

How have the ThinkLite inventors saved money on making and assembling their product?

Building a team

Finding the right people

Business is about working with people. You can't always do it all alone. Unless you want your invention to stay small, you'll need support. You may be a great thinker and good at building your gadget, but are you also good at  marketing and selling it? There are a lot of different skills required in making a product or business a success and it is unlikely that you'll be able to do everything. Think about the roles that you can do well and that you want to do, then think about those which are left over.

It's important that you have support for your idea and your team should be there to do this. Once you've listed the jobs that need filling, think about how to find the right people. It's always a good idea to find people who have experience within the industry you are planning to work in. You may want to advertise for people who have experience in launching gadgets or approach recruitment agencies that specialise in this area.

CHALLENGE

You want to focus on building your gadget and would rather other people focused on the money and selling side of the business. List the job roles that you'll need to complete your team.

Young Entrepreneur
AlterG

Sean Whalen (below) from Fremont, California, is the first to admit that his company, AlterG, owes a lot to his team, and especially his father. AlterG makes an anti-gravity treadmill that helps people recover from injuries. Robert Whalen, Sean's dad, was a NASA research scientist who originally invented the product over twenty years ago for use by astronauts. With the shutting down of the space programme, it might have been forgotten.

Years later, when Sean was at Stanford University, studying for a Masters' degree in entrepreneurship, he saw the possibilities for applying the invention to help athletes. The success of entering the sports market has given his business a turnover of $10 million, employing 50 people. Success has also come from working with high profile athletes, such as US footballer Oguchi Onyewu (who famously made a speedy recovery in time for the last World Cup in 2010). Their remarkable stories have attracted sales to hospitals to treat ordinary members of the public.

The success of AlterG has been down to building up a team of father, son and high profile athletes who have promoted sales.

YOUR THOUGHTS

What important role did Robert Whalen play in the team at AlterG?

Leading from the front

Staying in control

Once you've set up your team and are starting to get close to putting your new product on the market, you'll find that you are very busy. You'll have to learn to manage your time so you can think about important decisions. Although you might listen to others, the major decisions are likely to be yours. You will need to sharpen up your problem-solving skills. As the inventor, it's absolutely essential that you remain in control of what's going on, unless you decide to sell your invention of course; however, that's probably not likely just yet. There are several ways of making sure things stay ahead in the right direction.

Inspiring your team

The golden rule is that you can't do everything yourself. You've chosen the people in your team for the qualities they can bring to making your invention a success, so you must be able to trust them to get on with it. If everyone knows what their responsibilities are, you will find it much easier to inspire them to achieve the goals you have set. It might be a good idea to read up on how other inventors set about becoming team leaders. The common factor is usually that they made their team members believe they mattered, and gave them all clear, realistic objectives.

CHALLENGE

Make a list of all the things that make a good leader. Tick those that you think you have. Do you think you would have the leadership skills to make your gadget a success?

Young Entrepreneur
Anna Bullus

Anna Bullus (left) used to find that she was often wading through loads of sticky chewing gum on the streets. When Anna read that the UK spends over £150 million each year on cleaning up gum, she decided to do something about it. What's more, she reckoned that as chewing gum was made of a type of rubber, it could easily be recycled like rubber. After eight months in a laboratory, she came up with an answer. She created a material out of chewing gum (along with a secret ingredient) she called Bullus Recycled Gum Polymer (BRGP) which she then used to make bins for chewing gum: the Gumdrop. The Gumdrop is the world's first chewing gum bin made with your recycled gum. The bins are bright pink and strapped to lampposts in the street for passers-by to deposit their used gum. The gum is then collected and made into more Gumdrop bins.

As the inventor, Anna wanted control over her Bullus Recycled Gum Polymer and so she set up Gumdrop Ltd. The company was set up so that she could have complete control on how the Gumdrop bins are sold and marketed, but also the future use of the BRGP material. Already she has plans on using it to create Wellington boots, or gum boots!

YOUR THOUGHTS

Why do you think Anna makes a good leader?

Developing your marketing plan

Getting ready to sell

No matter how good your product and your team, you can't succeed without a clear blueprint for success. Draw up a marketing plan that includes every part of the marketing mix. The aim of the plan is for you to say how you are going to attract your target audiences to try out and buy your invention. And, of course, make sure the plan is closely linked to your budget.

Once you've decided on your plan, you need to put it into action. To do this, it's often helpful to think of the four Ps:

Product – what your product offers and what makes it different from its competition.

Price – what your customers will be happy to pay for the product.

Place – how and where you are going to sell your product – in shops, supermarkets, online or all three.

Promotion – how to reach your market most effectively. This can include advertising, direct mail and personal selling.

Is your promotional campaign a true reflection of your product?

NOBODY WILL DIE IN MOTORCYCLE ACCIDENTS ANY LONGER

CHALLENGE

You've decided to go ahead with your invention of child-friendly paints. Come up with a short marketing plan. Think about the four Ps.

Young Entrepreneur
Kathryn Gregory

Kathryn (KK) Gregory (right) from Bedford, Massachusetts invented Wristies in 1994 when she was only 10 years old. She found her wrists were hurting from the cold after building a snow fort. Doing some research told her there was nothing on the market that was going to solve the problem – so she became an inventor. Wristies are small fingerless gloves that are designed to be worn on their own or under other gloves to give extra protection in the cold winter months. They block the snow, wind and cold from slipping through those open gaps.

Her next step was to apply for a patent and trademark the name. Then she decided to set up a company to make and sell Wristies. Obviously, she needed to market them properly. KK's marketing plan was to follow what the experts say is always best to begin with: wear your product, use your product and talk about your product. Because of her age, it was a good media story and she got lots of publicity. She was able to build sales by selling online (she set up her website in 1996) as well as through shops.

YOUR THOUGHTS

What parts of the four Ps did KK use in her business?

Getting known

Standing out from the crowd

Does everyone know about your product? If you've done your research, you'll know who your target market is. Now you must find the best ways to reach it. This is known as a marketing strategy and usually involves advertising and other forms of promotion, such as publicity.

Advertising, promotion and publicity

Plan your advertising campaign, and support it with some promotional work, such as offering free samples. Advertising is often paid for and aims to get your product in the right media, either in print or online, to grab your customers' attention. Publicity can be free and means using events or promotions to make your product known. If your invention is very different then you should be able to get lots of news stories about it for free.

Young Entrepreneur

Tiffany Krumins

Tiffany Krumins (below) from Massachusetts founded Ava the Elephant in 2009 when she realised that there was a real need for a fun medicine dispenser for children. As someone who worked with special needs children, she understood that it wasn't really the taste of medicine that put children off, so much as the rather scary process of taking it. She checked and found nothing on the market that did the job.

So Tiffany got inventive and came up with Ava the Elephant as a special child-friendly way of encouraging the taking of medicine. But the really big break she got was appearing on the TV show *Shark Tank* that got her invention widely known. The resulting publicity was fantastic for her, as was the investment of $55,000 she received that enabled her to develop Ava as she wished. Now many people know something about her product.

YOUR THOUGHTS

How did Tiffany manage to get such good publicity?

Off with a bang!

Launch time

Right, you're ready at last. It's time to launch your gadget, and make as loud a noise as you can. You've got a great new invention that is meeting a real need, so you should be confident of success. But you can't always think of everything. Are things going according to plan? If there are any problems, be sure to put them right as quickly as possible, because first impressions really do count.

You may want to have a launch party. This would be a good chance to celebrate all the work you have done and make it a publicity event. In which case, think about the place, guests, entertainment, making your gadget centre stage and making sure that you have newspapers and the media there to cover it.

Social media networks and traditional methods

Social media networks must be buzzing with the date you've set to launch your product. In the same way, any advertising you do must be focused around the launch day. You need to get as many people interested in your gadget as possible. This is when you have a great chance to get people to try your invention, maybe for a special price, without putting your long-term plans at risk.

CHALLENGE

You want to launch the new app which gives people immediate access to family history details. What's your plan? Think about your target market.

Young Entrepreneurs
Instagram

When Kevin Systrom and Mike Krieger, from San Francisco, California launched Instagram in October 2010, they began one of the fastest ever success stories. Instagram is a photo-sharing app for smartphones, which helps users give an old-fashioned finish to their pictures in a simple, modern way, and then share them easily and quickly with friends and followers. Other similar apps have been invented, yet none have been quite so easy to use on social network sites.

In the build-up, the inventors managed to create an interest in the app by getting various friends and opinion-formers to give it a trial. They spread the word via social networks: there was no paid-for advertising or publicity, nor was there a big launch party. Instead Systrom and Krieger were in their offices on launch day to monitor and cope with demand. Even so, they were unprepared for the level of immediate success (Twitter creator Jack Dorsey tweeted the app to his legions of followers – so did Justin Bieber) and had to upgrade their systems to cope with the response, soon growing to 5 million photos uploaded each day. Within 18 months, Facebook bought the company for $1 billion.

YOUR THOUGHTS

Why didn't Instagram need any paid-for advertising when they launched?

Tracking sales and distribution

Are sales going to plan?

From the very first day of your invention's life in the outside world, check all the sales figures regularly and carefully. Are you in the right shops and on the best websites? There may be others you could switch to. Are your likely customers buying? There may be reasons putting them off. Are the targets you set achievable? Never be afraid to change things if they're not running smoothly. If you're using online sales, are you getting enough site visitors and are they then buying your invention?

It's important you are happy you're going through the right distribution channels.

Think about the kind of shops which are suitable for your product. Go to them with a sample and pay careful attention to their feedback.

They may be able to recommend other shops if they feel the product is unsuitable for them. Also, think about selling online: you can often make more money here by selling direct to customers, but you may have to charge for postage and if your invention is large, this could be expensive!

CHALLENGE A store orders 20 of your gadgets to sell, but wants exclusive rights in the area – meaning that no other store nearby can sell your product. Should you accept? Why?

Young Entrepreneur
ManCans

Hart Main (right) from Marysville, Ohio started making his candles scented with manly smells as a bit of a joke. His younger sister was selling candles for a school fair in November 2010 and he teased her that the scents were all too girly, and that there should be more designed to appeal to men. She laughed at the idea but he has proved her wrong by inventing ManCans with smells such as Sawdust, Coffee, Fresh Cut Grass, Campfire, Bacon, Grandpa's Pipe, New Mitt (baseball glove), New York Style Pizza and Dirt.

Just 14 years old, Hart started by visiting local shops, and although he had a few rejections, some buyers were interested and stocked the candles. Then he branched out and started to target some national shops, resulting in over 60 outlets now carrying his products. His next step was to set up a website, so that he could sell directly to customers. Candles are easy to package and post and most of his sales come from individual orders through his website.

YOUR THOUGHTS

How are ManCans gaining most sales?

Turning problems into gains

Always think positively

Don't be put off by problems. Nearly everyone has them at the start of their business careers. The important thing is to learn from them and your mistakes. Just make a few changes to your invention, your plan or your type of operation, and try again – the key is never to give up! You might even be able to use a problem to make things better. Keep trying different ways and means until you've got everything just how you want it.

A batch of your gadgets get delivered damaged. What should you do so as not to disappoint the customer?

This is the real world, and nobody expects things to be perfect. An important person falls ill, there's a power cut affecting your online sales, a van breaks down or there's a strike in your neighbourhood: some things are out of your control, just try to get round them as best you can.

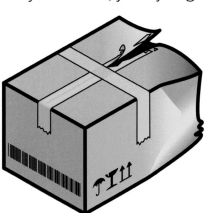

One of the important things to remember is you must always let your customers know if there are going to be any delays or changes in the plan. A simple message on your website, or by phone, text or email will save you a lot of bother later and could gain you a lot of goodwill.

CHALLENGE

The battery power for your portable iron only lasts nine hours when advertised to last for ten hours. This has only been noticed by a few of your customers. What do you do?

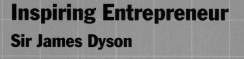

Inspiring Entrepreneur
Sir James Dyson

Sir James Dyson (left) from Norfolk, England has given his name to one of the most famous vacuum cleaners in the world. Yet his start in business wasn't an easy one, even once he'd come up with his invention. People in the vacuum cleaner business did not like the idea of a bagless vacuum cleaner but he used this as his selling point. It took 10 years but he got there eventually.

He had tried to launch his special cleaner in 1983 on the grounds that it would not lose suction as it continued to pick up dirt. But because his model had no bags, the industry in the UK managed to stop it being stocked because people would no longer buy replacement bags. This was a big setback: however he realised the UK was not the only country where he could sell. So he launched it in Japan, won an International Design Prize, and re-launched it in the UK in 1993. This time his advertising slogan was 'Say goodbye to the bag', appealing directly to customers. It worked, giving him a global brand – and he has never looked back.

YOUR THOUGHTS

Do you think Dyson cleaners would have been as successful without the setback?

So what's next?

Planning for the future

Brilliant – your hard work has been rewarded with success! Everyone seems to want your gadget, and you're making a profit even faster than you planned. But don't stop there. Use your inventive mind to come up with new ideas or think of ways in which you can build on that success and expand your business. Don't be afraid to think big now you know how it's done. Within reason, of course: remember you can't do everything at once.

SUCCESS ▶

CHALLENGE

Now that your app for delivering family history details is a success, what else could you develop in this area?

New products and inventions are springing up all the time, and you must make sure you're always planning carefully what you're going to do next. There are ways in which you can do this without taking too much of a risk. Probably you'll find that once you've gone through the excitement of inventing your own gadget and taking it out into the world, you'll want to do it all over again soon. Only even better.

Inspiring Entrepreneur
Steve Jobs

Steve Jobs from San Francisco, California was not the only genius involved in the electronics company Apple but he was the one who made sure it was always looking forward. The way he did this was by continually reinventing Apple and its products, so that there was always something new just around the corner. He started Apple with Steve Wozniak in 1976, but after the launch of the Apple Mac in 1984, he left after a disagreement. He learned from his mistake.

Steve Jobs
1955-2011

YOUR THOUGHTS

How did Steve Jobs keep Apple moving ahead?

Jobs returned in 1996, when Apple bought the company he'd set up and he was determined as an entrepreneur to use the company's inventors wisely. The key was to invent simple gadgets, adapted to current lifestyles: he realised that highly attractive design and smooth functioning would together bring customer loyalty. It was the introduction of the iMac in 1998 which took them to the next level of success. Since then the launch of the iPod (2001), the setting up of iTunes (2003), the 2008 introduction of the iPhone and the iPad unveiling (2010) have all kept the company at the forefront. Other rivals tried to compete but Apple products were always more stylish and appealing to customers.

Glossary

advertising Images or stories that interest people in your product.

app Short for application. A useful gadget you download to your mobile phone.

backers People who lend you money to help you start your business.

blueprint The original plan for marketing (or creating) your invention.

budget The amount of money you expect to spend (and receive).

cash flow The money coming in and going out.

costs Everything you must spend to make sales.

distribution Where your products go in order to be sold.

efficient Something that is working well.

entrepreneur Someone who takes a financial risk in order to make a profit.

fault A problem with how your gadget or invention works.

feedback Comments on what you've said, made or done.

financial plans Estimates of how much money you need and how much you'll make.

forefront In a position that really stands out.

function What something (or someone) does.

infringement Going over the line of what you're normally allowed to do (– can be illegal).

inspire Set a great example that people want to copy.

inventor Someone who creates a new gadget or product.

investors People who put money into your business.

jackpot The biggest prize in a competition or lottery.

laboratory A place to conduct scientific experiments.

launch The moment you open your business or start selling your product.

manufacturer Someone who makes a product.

market A group of potential customers (or place where they gather).

marketing mix The things you must do to market your goods.

marketing plan Describing your likely customers and how you'll sell to them.

market research Finding out if there's a market for your idea, or how it's doing.

patent The legal right to be the only producer of what you've invented.

persistence The ability to keep going.

primary research Finding new information that is collected for the first time.

profit The amount of money you receive for sales, less the cost of making them.

prototype The original version of your invention.

publicity The ways you get your business noticed in the media.

risk The chance of losing money invested in a business.

rivals Everyone who is competing with you to sell to consumers.

running costs The money you need to keep your business going.

sales figures The total amount of sales reported regularly.

secondary research Finding information that already exists.

social media The recent inventions that help you connect to other people.

social networking Connecting with other people through social media.

software Programmes for electronic devices (such as PCs and mobile phones).

target audience The people you want to hear the messages about your products.

target market The people you want to interest in buying your products.

upgrade An improvement you make to your product.

urther information

Websites of featured entrepreneurs

terG **www.alter-g.com/**

rticheke **www.youtube.com/watch?v=Y21FU-zHQtU**

nna Bullus **www.gumdropbin.com/**

r Robert Dyson **www.dyson.co.uk/**

ill Gates **www.microsoft.com/en-us/news/exec/billg**

assidy Goldstein **www.bkfk.com/product/crayonholder**

stagram **http://instagr.am/**

teve Jobs **www.apple.com/**

Tiffany Krumins **http://avatheelephant.co.uk/**

Makin' Bacon **www.makinbacon.com/**

ManCans **http://man-cans.com/**

PetLawn **http://thepetlawn.com/**

Storymaker, Storyteller **www.littleriot.co.uk/**

ThinkLite **www.thinklite.com/**

Trunki **www.trunki.com/**

Wristies **www.wristies.com/**

Other websites

ww.bbc.co.uk/dragonsden/

fficial website of the *Dragons' Den* programme where you can see other
udding entrepreneurs and the advice they receive.

ww.ideafinder.com/features/classact/young.htm

eatures a list of young inventors who have made a difference to our lives.

ww.youngentrepreneur.com/

nline forum for information and advice on being a young entrepreneur.

Books

he *Top Ten: Inventions that Changed the World* by Chris Oxlade (Franklin Watts, 2009)

Weird True Facts: Inventions by Moira Butterfield (Franklin Watts, 2012)

ote to parents and teachers: every effort has been made by the
ublishers to ensure that these websites are suitable for children,
nd that they contain no inappropriate or offensive material. However,
ecause of the nature of the Internet, it is impossible to guarantee that
he contents of these sites will not be altered.

Index

advertising 30, 32, 34, 35, 39
AlterG 27
Apple 41
apps 18, 19, 20, 34, 35, 40
ArtiCheke 19
Ava the Elephant 33
awards 14, 15, 17, 19, 39

backers 14, 15, 24
Balsz, Dylan 21
Bendable Bike 15
budgets 14, 30
Bullus, Anna 29

company (starting your own) 9, 28, 29
costs 14, 15, 16, 24
Crayon Holder 13

development, product 20-21, 24
distribution 36
Dyson, James 39

Erikson, Annika 19

Fleck Abbey 23
funding 14–15, 23

Gates, Bill 11
Goldstein, Cassidy 13
grants 14
Gregory, Kathryn 31
Gumdrop 29

ideas 8, 9, 10, 11, 12–13, 14, 16, 18
Instagram 35

Jobs, Steve 41

Krieger, Mike 35
Krumins, Tiffany 33

launches 20, 34–35
Law, Rob 9

Main, Hart 37
Makin' Bacon 23
ManCans 37
marketing 8, 12, 26, 29, 30–31, 32, 33
Microsoft 11
Montgomery, Joanna 17

networks, social media 34, 35

online selling 31, 37

patents 8, 9, 22, 23, 28, 33
PetLawn 21
plans, financial 14, 24–25
promotion 32, 33
prototypes 9, 14, 16, 18, 20
publicity 15, 23, 24, 31, 32, 33, 34, 35

research, market 18–19, 20

sales 24, 25, 27, 36, 37
Scott, Kevin 15
set-backs 38–39
Shark Tank 33
Smith, Tilden 21
Storymaker, Storyteller 17
Systrom, Kevin 35

team, the 26–27, 28, 30
ThinkLite 25
Trunki 9

vacuum cleaners 16, 39

Wadhwani, Dinesh 25
Whalen, Sean 27

Wozniak, Steve 41
Wristies 31